IT'S JUST A
PHASE

"Journaling with The Moon"

STEPHANIE POWERS

It's Just a Phase
Journaling with the moon

To request permissions, contact the publisher
at spowers@lightworkers-lounge.com

ISBN: 979-8-41979-966-0

First paperback edition February 2022.

Cover art by Jennifer Stimson

For Pau, who I'm sure I've known in many lives.

Your Cancer moon has nurtured my Chiron in
Cancer more than you'll ever know.

Thank you for introducing me to my big
three that fateful day in January.

Lightworkers
Lounge

Acknowledgments

I feel so lucky to live in both a country and day and age where we can self-publish whatever we want. That creative freedom is something I thank the sun, moon and stars for everyday.

With this said, self-publishing a book without a publisher takes a lot of time, money, faith, and a village of people to support you. Even with that, it still takes immense fortitude and tenacity to pour so much effort and money into something you aren't sure will return your investment.

Lightworkers Lounge Community — you come first. You are the reason I am able to self-publish. Thank you so much for following my life's story with an open mind and heart, and allowing me to assist you in your journey. I still can't fully digest the magnitude of your love and support for me. I get 'truth bumps' every time I read a letter or DM of gratitude. All I can say is… thank you. So much.

To the love of my life, JL, Baby J, Jordan… thank you for passionately supporting me from the moment we virtually met. For buying half a dozen of every new product or service I release, just because. For knowing my highest self better than I do, and pushing me towards her everyday. This book would never be what it is without you as my foundation, so thank you. I love you endlessly. Of course you bring me a salad as I'm typing this, as you know I forget to eat. My angel.

Sara, my muff! Thank you for using that Virgo eye and Gemini precision to proofread this book. I will always see you as a professional editor, and most of all, a professional best friend; there's no one like you. I've been searching for another human with a rainbow aura like yours… still nothing.

To my mother and my brother, my tribe. My family. We may be small but boy is our love big. Mama, thank you for raising me in true Aquarius fashion and allowing me to be whoever I wanted. I can only imagine how many times you wanted to caution me otherwise, but told me to go for it. I owe my life's work to you.

And Ben, the moment I sent you the first proof of the cover and you said "I've always been super proud to have a sister who is a published author!" — I knew I found my purpose. Thank you.

Contents

I think I was eight years old when I began thumbing through the Sunday paper, throwing the coupon section over to mom, and searching for the hidden treasure amongst thin pages of black and white text...**my horoscope.**

Will my crush like me back this week? Will I make new friends? Will I go on an adventure somewhere far away this year? I couldn't wait to find out.

Astrology is the study of the stars.

How romantic does that sound? Aside from the whimsical romanticism of studying the night sky, I can't say exactly why I'm drawn to it — it's just something that has always felt right. Is it that the career point (MC) in my chart is in Aquarius, who rules Astrology? Perhaps. But most importantly, a lot of people turn to Astrology when they feel knocked off their divine purpose, lost, and in need of a map home. Me being one of them.

In my prior job as a Health Coach, I used to tell clients:

You know how to eat healthy.
You know you need to drink water and exercise.

So why aren't you doing it?

You're born knowing your purpose. Knowing what you love. Knowing what mark you came to leave on the world...It never leaves you.

So why aren't you doing it?

Somewhere along the way, during our most formative years, society, family, media, all shoot arrow after arrow of influential energy that stacks continuous barriers between your mind and your soul… and you *forget*.

You forget who you are, because you're conditioned to wrap your identity around being *something*. A sister, daughter, wife, mother. A brother, son, husband, father. Anything but your unique self. And then this forgetfulness manifests as anxiety, depression, operating from an external locus of control, affecting everything from your career to your relationships….and down, down we go.

I find a lot of people who study the stars have anxiety. It's true! I used to have anxiety so crippling, I convinced myself I had a brain tumor and couldn't drive. Anxiety is a fear of the future. It's built up energy from the powerful thoughts of feeling like you aren't in control of anything. I was a child who didn't have a lot of stability growing up. It's no wonder I reached for the stars; I was desperate for anything to tell me how the movie ends, so I knew what to expect and could brace myself.

Now, as an Astrologer, I find it funny that I haven't read my personal horoscope in years. It just doesn't appeal to me in the way it used to. It's also because at 33 I've finally learned some practical ways to use my anxiety as a super power rather than a burden. It's important to get clear with ourselves on why we're studying Astrology before we dive in, because as is with everything in life, too much of anything can be a bad thing.

Astrology is a beautiful way to, 'predict the weather' but it should not be something you center your entire life around. Let it be a tool, not a foundation.

* * *

Your Birth Chart is a screenshot of where all the planets were in the sky the moment you were born. The first breath you filled your new lungs with...where was the Moon? The Sun? Venus? This is what your natal birth chart will reveal to you.

I want to preface this work book with the idea that Astrology requires you to practice non-attachment. It is silly to imagine that we could categorize our entire human species into 12 signs.

To each sign, house, and planet, there is a high road and a low road. An evolved and unevolved side; two ways everything can go. This is why no two Scorpios are the same. Why one Aries is a wild, athletic extrovert, and one hasn't touched a ball or left the house.

I want to reiterate as well, that there is no such thing as a bad placement in Astrology. Of course, there are easy and difficult placements. But I often find people with 'difficult' placements in their natal chart, tend to enjoy some of the richest emotional rewards life can offer. Like the happiest, most optimistic elder you've ever met who has seen more death and heartache imaginable. But, chose to turn it into an appreciation for all of the little things in life. We would never know the ecstasy of joy if we hadn't experienced the depths of pain.

Everyone's birth chart is unique to them, like a thumb print. Some people will enjoy having a Leo moon; being the life of the party and love any occasion to have friends over. While others with a Leo moon, who, say, were raised in a household where they were not free to express themselves, will be just the opposite: shy and introverted. Even in the case of twins with identical birth charts, they could have different personalities depending upon how they perceived the world and life events around them, and whether or not they chose to 'paddle up stream' with their chart, or flow with the current they were dealt.

With this workbook, keep an open, flexible mind. Take a deep breath in, and long exhale before you dive in. Repeat a few times, until you feel grounded.

Should you proceed in this workbook with intuition up and judgment down, be prepared to call yourself out. To really gaze at who you've become in the metaphorical mirror. Be prepared to cry, have deep realizations, and sudden epiphanies. Prepare to shed a layer (or four) of your current personality, in a matter of 30 days. *I suppose this book will be like a psychological, spiritual cleanse.*

Who are you taking information from?

I think it's important to know who we take information from. Especially in today's age of over abundance in people becoming self-proclaimed gurus and specialists, having no formal education or earth shattering transformations. One of my podcast episodes called 'Toxic Psychology on Instagram' is still one of our most downloaded.

Projecting. Ever heard of it? This is when someone is giving advice based off of their past experiences. We all do it. It's quite natural. You're projecting right now as you read this. Everything you've been through, the trauma, happy times, are all influencing how you perceive the text in this book. What will you remember? And what will blow in the wind? Your subconscious combined with all of your past experiences will decide.

Authors, Podcasters, Teachers...they are projecting information from their own past experiences that may not match what you've been through or where you're going. It's all about the vibration each teacher is sending out. Does it match yours? You'll often find that your life may mirror the life of your favorite spiritual guide, because you will often share the same frequency due to similar past experiences.

After over 1 million downloads and 250+ episodes of my podcast, Lightworkers Lounge, I've come to find that I can have some of the most world renowned, highly talented guests, but their downloads won't hold a candle to someone who is less well known, but pours energy and soul into their message. Someone who emanates the frequency of a healer, rather than a teacher, will almost always be a crowd favorite. They've usually been through some shit. We've all been through some shit! But how we choose to alchemize it, or, *turn that poison into medicine*, will greatly influence our teaching style.

That's why, I'd like to share a little bit about who I am and where I come from, so you know what angles I'm projecting at you from.

* * *

I'm what you'd call a, 'military brat' without ever having a family member in the military. I've moved around the United States so frequently in my life, when people ask me where I'm from I simply say with a smirk: *Earth.*

Born in Southern Indiana, raised in New Hampshire, attended University everywhere from Las Vegas to Miami, I spent my first marriage in the Carolinas and fulfilled my dreams of living in the Florida Keys a few times. There have been stints in Colorado, Texas, and even a motorhome for a year. I truly don't know what culture I most resonate with. East Coast or West Coast. New England or the South. It's beautiful, liberating, and oh so free. I have been blessed to spend Winters in the Caribbean and Summers in the San Juan Mountains. As lucky as I've been, it can really leave one feeling as though they don't fit in or belong anywhere. I have struggled greatly with loneliness and isolation as a result.

It's like being on the playground at recess; when the bell rings, we line up with the other kids in our class (family) and we all have a classroom (hometown) assigned to us, where we go to continue our day. Only, I don't have a classroom. And because I spend so much time alone at recess, skipping on the lectures inside, I don't have any classmates, either. While everyone returns to their assigned rooms, I aimlessly wander the empty halls, occasionally peaking through the glass into a classroom door, wondering what it's like to have a desk and a cubby to call your own.

I was raised by a single mother. She is so loving and powerful, that I never missed having a male figure in my life. My biological father struggles with alcoholism amongst other mental health issues, and I have never had a relationship with him. In fact, the word 'dad' or 'father' feels like a foreign word rolling off my lips. I've had to retrain the muscles in my tongue to pronounce it, because they are so weakened by never voicing it. My mother never remarried; some decent men came into my life but were usually gone as soon as they came. None of them taught me anything about harnessing the power of masculinity. I've struggled with being financially independent, setting boundaries, and standing brave in the face of conflict as a result.

My mother sure tried her best, though. In fact, I would say she is 90% masculine, 10% feminine. A true phoenix, she went from raising us alone on welfare, to securing her masters degree and showering us with abundance. To this day I've never met anyone with tenacity and patience like her.

Inheriting my Aquarius mother's dominant masculinity traits, shortly after college I married an Aquarius boy I met in 3rd grade, and moved to the Carolinas with our two cats and nothing else. We knew no one. As a way to block the heavy influence of people who just wanted the best for us, we lied to our family and friends, saying we had jobs down there waiting for us. We didn't. And very little money or family support, either. We simply knew it was the right thing to do. And as it does, the Universe provided; within a week of arriving to Charlotte, North Carolina, we both had full time jobs with great benefits. North and South Carolina will always be my safe haven and sanctuary.

While this chapter of life felt very safe and certain, I also went through some of the darkest, loneliest years of my life. A true dark night of the soul, if you will. It wasn't even a year of us living in Charlotte that I received a diagnosis at a routine checkup that would change my life forever. I was diagnosed with Hyperthyroid and the autoimmune disease, Hashimoto's.

The Endocrinologist I was referred to told me I wouldn't be able to conceive a child without intervention, and asked if I wanted to remove my entire thyroid next week. My weakened intuition was usually a whisper, but in this moment, it was a piercing roar. I knew all of those statements were exaggerated, and intuitively knew this health issue was more energetic than it was physical. That day was the biggest wake up call of my life.

Aside from my then-husband, I had no one to share this news with. And seeing as I worked from home, I had no co-workers to talk to, either. At the time, my brother was diagnosed with chronic epilepsy, and my mother was caught up both physically and emotionally helping him, so I didn't want to bother her.

It was through forced isolation and self-reflection after the diagnosis, that I came to the difficult realization, *I was living my life completely wrong. Backwards. Paddling up stream.* If my birth chart said go right, I was running, full speed, to the left.

I had followed what everyone else expected of me: the safe route. The route of easy acceptance by others, because life never felt safe or certain growing up. People in my life, places where we lived, it was always a matter of "when" not "if" they would disappear.

* * *

Four years later, I naturally healed my autoimmunity without any Western intervention. Feeling inspired and empowered by this, I decided to take the biggest risk of my life; leave the predictable, corporate 9-5 and become a Certified Holistic Health Coach, working for myself. I published my first book called Thyroid First Aid Kit to share how I healed myself with nothing but diet/lifestyle changes. It's still selling in multiple countries today.

My then husband and I moved to Denver, Colorado in November 2017. The crippling anxiety had melted away, I was in love with my career as a Health Coach, but I still felt as though I was paddling up stream in some area of life…

Just five short years into marriage, I found myself taking a separate car to a courthouse, trailing behind a man I thought I knew, to file for divorce.

That man was my best friend. We got on so well, and practically grew up together. We never fought, which I used to wear like a badge of honor. But I quickly realized that conflict in a relationship is healthy, if not, a necessity. Healthy conflict means you are continuously setting boundaries, avoiding codependence, and sharing what makes you happy and what doesn't, keeping the relationship thriving. We never did any of this. Just two kids, trauma bonded to the silent safety of one another.

So on a warm Spring morning, when he walked 10 feet ahead of me and let the door to the courthouse slam in my face, I knew It was a good run — but this is why it had to end. We signed the final papers for the divorce on the exact day of our five year wedding anniversary, June 1st. The day my Saturn Return began.

Where one relationship ends, another always begins. Where one person is excused from a seat at our table, a new, better aligned person will inevitably come to sit down. It was around this same time that I met one of my best friends, Paulina, though the most serendipitous moment at a dog park, early one cold January morning. It was her who introduced me to my moon and rising sign, and I was hooked; both on her Astrology knowledge, and the effortless connection that I had never felt with a friend before.

With each cup of tea she made me in her apartment, I felt so nurtured. It seems like such a simple, cordial thing to do. But I had not had any socialization in years. This was such a treat for me; my slow re-entry into the world of being social. Every week, as I left my top floor apartment and hopped down the stairs in my socks to her first floor apartment, we would cozy up and talk about our birth charts, our family's, the charts of men we've loved, and watched our dogs play.

As I was enduring the awkward, slow burn of splitting up from someone I had known for over a decade, walking into the safety of Pau's apartment, I finally felt something I hadn't felt in years.... *Home. Safe.*

By 29 I was divorced, living out of an old Subaru I purchased on a whim, and bouncing between Telluride and Key West. I was in the worst financial situation of my life, nowhere near where someone about to enter their thirties should be, but living in two of the most exquisite areas in the country. *Anything is possible.* Although I was not monetarily abundant, air bnb hopping with people I don't remember, those were some of the happiest days of my life. I felt so free. Finally on track. I finally stopped running left, and was turning my head to the right, lacing up my sneakers getting ready to go.

It was then that I created Lightworkers Lounge.

The high I felt in leaving the wrong marriage quickly diffused into the reality of all the healing that lay in front of me— I have a dog, I do not have a home, and I am years away from securing a steady stream of income with my new business. *What the fuck have I done.*

As the dust from the explosion of divorce started to settle, I thought I would be able to just sweep it all away, and instantly be met with a beautiful, clean home that had gardenias growing around the white picket fence, paired with a perfect partner who read my mind and catered to my every want and need.

But all I could see was a war-torn village. Everything burnt to the ground with some ashes still ablaze. My heart was free. But with the realization that divorce is caused by two people, not one — now it was time to clean up and rebuild. *Kinda forgot about that part.*

So with embarrassment, at 29 years old, I moved back into my old childhood bedroom with my mother in New Hampshire. Tail tucked between my legs, I promised myself I would temporarily rest here to financially, but most importantly, emotionally recuperate and heal from the divorce.

I went to yin yoga classes every Thursday night at the base of a mountain. I attended monthly women's full moon circles, which drastically inspired my love for the stars and their potent healing power. And of course, I immersed myself in weekly therapy sessions.

It was a sad, yet transformative time for me. I was introduced to parts of myself I never knew; both good and bad. I was reminded of the importance of community and connection. I never thought I would say this, but sometimes I miss those cold days in New England. I really grew into who I am today.

Although I wasn't making a dime from it, I treated Lightworkers Lounge as though it was my full time job during this time. Clocking in at 9AM, and clocking out at 5PM. Taking an hour lunch. My audience was a mere 25 people. But giving this much energy to it, and trusting the Universe, it started to grow by nearly 2,000 people every few days. It reached heights I never once imagined it would.

Eight months into my stint at moms, I was financially back on my feet and emotionally ready to get back out there. I drove across the country to Telluride, eager to spend a Summer in the San Juan Mountains. It was as beautiful as you'd imagine. After that, I felt confident enough to take another chance at making my Florida Keys dream come true. Sure enough, by following strong synchronicities, I ended up living in an old tree house in The Keys for the Fall and

Winter seasons. To this day, it was one of the happiest, luckiest chapters of my life. *I did what everyone told me I could never do, but what I always knew was right for me.*

While I lived in the sunshine state, fulfilling my dream of being a permanent resident of the Keys, something happened I never saw coming; I fell in love with a man from Texas.

I'm still not sure what's more odd about it. The fact that I found someone who checks off all the boxes I've ever had, and constantly challenges me to become better...*or that he's from Texas.* With a Scorpio moon that matches mine, I knew from the moment we ruined the friendship with a kiss... it was game over.

In February the following year, I reluctantly packed up my clothes in a trash bag, left the treehouse, and headed to Austin, Texas. The thousands of followers I amassed through sharing my personal life on Instagram were sending me messages of hesitation. Wondering why I would leave the thing I worked so hard for. But, what I didn't share was things at the treehouse started to get tough. Real tough. I was working with no wifi, using a hotspot to upload podcast episodes. My laptop's motherboard broke down from the salty air getting inside. And although I was slowly saving up enough for an apartment, the cost of living down in the islands was increasing faster than my income.

After a long four months of washing dishes in a tiny bathroom sink, having a shower that only stays warm for a couple of minutes, and cooking outside with mosquitos, I started to crave modern commodities. The thought of, with the income I was currently making, I could easily afford an apartment somewhere up in the mainland, really started to eat at me. With a giant garden tub and a working kitchen sans bugs, I started to seriously weigh my options. The Keys were my dream, but not in a tiny treehouse that didn't have a sink to wash dishes in. My partner visited me a few times, and he often mentioned how wild it was that I was running an entire community from that environment. I knew it was time to go.

When you combine the chemical concoction of new love with the desperation for living in a modern world, you get an island girl driving to Texas, tears as salty as the ocean streaming down her face, bidding farewell to the dream she just can't seem to hold tight enough to keep forever.

It wasn't goodbye, it was be right back.

Life with him has been both everything I wanted, and everything I didn't know I wanted. Our life together is chock full of adventure, soul development, and most of all, passionate love only fit for the movies. I've never had anyone support my dreams as much as he has. And as if you couldn't have guessed; we eventually left Texas and moved back to Florida. This time, in a real house, with bedrooms, a bath tub, and a kitchen sink. *Abundance.*

Feeling more settled and aligned than ever in my life, I decided to take Debra Silverman's Applied Astrology course to further my studies. I completed Level 2 when I decided it was time to go live and give birth chart readings via zoom. The moon sign was always, and still is, my favorite. It rules our emotional selves, and I believe that is the control center for absolutely everything we do. So powerful!

Although it's not the easiest placement for one to have, I have my moon in Scorpio, and thoroughly believe it to be the best part about me. I'm fiercely loyal, I don't get triggered by much because of that Scorpio thirst for psychology, and yes — I will go to the grave with your secrets.

* * *

So, there you have it. The energy behind the words you are about to read.

Can you guess my big three by that short autobiography?

Sagittarius Sun
Scorpio moon
Taurus rising

My Mercury is also in Sagittarius, so throughout this workbook it will be all about the big picture. The forest.

It will be your job to decode the trees.

The Moon

I like to tell my clients that we play three different characters every day:

Your sun sign, moon sign, and your rising sign.

Our moon character is one of the most important signs to understand when coming back to ourselves. When understanding why you do the things you do. Representing our emotional body, your moon sign will tell you who you become when "shit hits the fan."

If you're a water moon, (Scorpio, Pisces, Cancer) your initial reaction to emotionally intense situations may be to cry, or isolate yourself to calm down. If you're an Earth moon (Virgo, Capricorn, Taurus) you will be the one to calm everyone down, handling the situation with a steady hand and practicality. If you're an air moon (Aquarius, Gemini, Libra) you will want to talk about what just happened. And if you're a fire moon (Sagittarius, Leo, Aries) well, you might just be the one who started the drama and certainly won't back down without a fight.

If the moon represents our emotional core, that would tell us that this sign in our birth chart really runs the entire show! We wake up and decide what to eat based off of how we feel. We choose life partners based off of how they make us feel. We choose career aspirations because they make us *feel* a certain way, whether it's financially secure or passionate. *The moon sign is very important!*

I once read that the moon sign in our birth chart not only represents our emotional realm, but it represents the way we view our mothers. (or the feminine energy that raised us) Remember earlier when I mentioned that I watched my mother raise my brother and I on welfare, to being financially abundant with a masters degree? The example my mother always set for me was a phoenix rising from the ashes. Big transformational energy. The sign that rules transformation? Scorpio. My moon.

The moon is, most importantly, the true test of romantic compatibility!

Ah, yes. I hate to be the bearer of bad news, but every time you meet a new romantic interest, I wouldn't advise comparing your sun signs to measure compatibility. If the sun sign represents ego, our logical mind, and the moon sign represents heart and soul, what we need to feel emotionally satisfied, which do we want to compare with someone? Are we looking for our ego mate? *Or our soulmate?*

The Sun sign comes out when we're with our friends and family; the people who know us, our quirks, what to talk about and what to avoid… they know our ego personality.

The Moon sign comes out when we're alone or with a romantic partner. I always like to ask my clients; if you're on a long road trip by yourself, what kind of music do you gravitate towards? Podcasts? Audiobooks? These are a reflection of your moon sign.

I think most of us can agree that who we are with friends is inherently different than who we are alone with a lover. *(Besides for if your sun and moon are the same, of course.)* Perhaps when we're out with girlfriends, we are wild, funny, extroverted. But when we're at home with our romantic partner, maybe we veer towards being more serious, introverted and sensual.

I'll never forget the most blatant example of how differing my sun and moon signs are. I'm a Sagittarius sun; the Bachelorette of the zodiac. The wild child, with a laugh that can be heard across the Atlantic. My life motto has always been, "Don't fence me in." Yet, there I was, with a man down on one knee in front of me on the brink of my 22nd birthday, saying yes to a proposal for marriage. That doesn't seem very Sagittarius... *does it?*

To understand why I would find myself in such a predicament, I look to my Scorpio moon. Ruling the deepest level of devotion and commitment to someone, committing my heart & soul to another seems like the only way to love. Needless to say, I have never dated casually. I mate for life. Ending my marriage was one of the most difficult things I've ever had to do. But it was not because of the fear of heartbreak. In the words of Evelyn Hugo, it was because of "fear of failure of the relationship." Realizing that there was no devotion on either end. *"There has to be love in order to have heartbreak."*

Our emotions control everything we do. They are the true command center of our life. Therefore, it is safe to say that the commander in chief of our natal chart, is our moon sign. The Sun has a strong influence too, of course, but in this age of Aquarius we find ourselves in, people are starting to omit logical, egotistical thinking (Sun) and follow their heart and intuition. (Moon)

The moon changes signs every 2-2.5 days. She moves fast! And knowing that the moon controls all of our emotional centers, our mental state moves just as fast — right along with it.

Moon journaling is something that I'm sure has been created before, but it was something I came up with on a personal level after my Astrology studies, to help decode my many personality flavors of the month. Female hormones aside, I often found myself swinging between many moods on a mild level, and I became curious as to why...

Aside from the usual monthly suspects: hormones, diet, and, well, life… I knew there was something beyond what my five senses could comprehend, affecting my emotional well being. And I knew that with a little knowledge and awareness, just like my history with anxiety, I had the power to control it and use it to my benefit.

Moon journaling is simple; everyday you check what sign the moon is in when you wake up. Like a weather forecast, if we know today it's supposed to be chilly, we will plan to wear a sweater and socks. If we know it's supposed to rain, we will pack an umbrella, and probably not do much with our hair.

If we know tomorrow the moon enters the sign of Libra, we may choose to finally go on a date, or clear the air with our lover. If the moon is in Capricorn, we may choose to schedule more work activities than normal or implement more self-discipline in our lives.

Each tropical zodiac sign has a generic description, but journaling for yourself can assist you in zoning in on which moon phases are more favorable for you, and which ones you need to 'pack an umbrella' for.

I've often found that the moon cycles we emotionally struggle with are typically the ones that are lit up in our natal chart through a stellium *(three or more planets in one house)* the house our sun sign occupies, or any area where a planet lies, injecting energy into that area of life. This is an indication that more attention is needed here. If you have a lot of planetary activity in the 4th house, you are really being called to heal a mother wound. To heal your feminine side, and break generational patterns. If you find a lot of planetary energy in the 7th house, you really came here to master the art of relationships, especially a union with one person.

Moon journaling can be like receiving test results back and finding out you're low on vitamin C. You will then supplement with food until your levels are normal. If you find Aries moon phases tend to turn you into the incredible hulk, perhaps for the next 30 day moon cycle you practice releasing anger more. Get more physical and move your body! See how you feel the next time the moon is in Aries.

Later in this workbook, I will walk you through what the moon in each sign could mean for you. I strategically use the word 'could' because to each placement, remember, there is an evolved side and an unevolved side. Depending on what life is currently like in that particular phase, each moon's influence could change.

For the sake of keeping this journal simple and user friendly to the Astro-Beginner, we are going to exclude detailed moon phases such as waxing crescent, waning crescent, etc. — take those into account once you've fully digested what each moon phase means for you.

Astrology is truly like learning a second language. Try not to be frustrated if none of it makes sense, or if as soon as you wake up tomorrow you forget everything you learned. Like a second language, you have to use it or you lose it! Keep practicing. Keep coming back to your moon journal every month. Eventually, through enjoyed repetition, the pasta will stick to the wall.

New Moon

I'm sure you've seen the posts all over social media by spiritual influencers discussing the potency of the new moon. But what does this mean?

A New Moon is when we can't see the moon in the sky; it is completely dark. No sun shining on it. Clean slate. (Also a great time to gaze at stars, with no light pollution from the moon!) A new moon is when the moon is in complete hiding. It's in the sky, but we can't see it.

During a new moon phase, Astrologers and Spiritualists alike have agreed through both study and experience, that it's a prosperous time to call in 'new' things.

New relationships
New beginnings
New home
New career moves

New friendships… whatever you feel your life is lacking, now is a great time to get the ball rolling to manifest and call it into your reality. Ever heard of a vision board? Dream board? Or of course, even a Pinterest board. The energy of a new moon is a great time to begin fantasizing about what it is you want to create in the next 30 day moon cycle.

Does this mean in the next month you will fall pregnant? Find the love of your life? Buy your dream house? Maybe! You never truly know. Just like the weather forecast; sometimes we see rain in the seven day forecast but as soon as the day comes, it's sunny. Most of the time, the new moon is simply a magnetic moment to 'start the snowball' that will turn into a snowman. If we keep our frequency aligned with the feeling of receiving whatever it is we desire, and constantly bounce the ball when the Universe throws it our way in the court of life, *you're destined to receive.*

Full Moon

The most popular moon phase of them all. What's not to love about a big, yellow, glowing ball in the sky? No matter what your spiritual or religious beliefs are, a full moon is something we can all agree is worth stopping to appreciate. It's one of life's many natural gifts, and to take a moment out of our day to stop and stare at a full moon in all it's glory is truly a blessing. It's mesmerizing.

I remember when I lived in Isle of Palms, South Carolina, I used to go to the beach every month on the full moon to watch it rise over the horizon of the Atlantic ocean. As the weather started to warm up, it became a Full Moon beach party with people of all ages coming to watch this natural phenomenon. It always warmed my heart to see that something so natural as a 'glowing rock' could bring us all together, if even for a small moment in time. Think of the power in that.

A Full moon is a time to release. Let go. Just the opposite of a new moon that wants to manifest something brand new, a full moon says "times up —the glass is FULL! Time to pour it out and start all over again with a new cycle."

A full moon is a time when we are all feeling… full. This could be in a good way, where we feel full of love and make incredible memories with our friends and family. Or, it could mean we are feeling *too* full and, one more drop in our cup could make emotions spill over and explode.

Ask any police officer, teacher, emergency room nurse, what their shift is like during a full moon. The vast majority of them will have plenty of stories about going to work on a full moon because the eight hour shift is usually filled with absolute madness from start to finish. The police officer receives double the calls. The teacher couldn't calm the children down if she diffused 3lbs of lavender oil. The nurse is simply short staffed because there's not enough hands to heal the people piling in. We all go a bit mad under the full moon's influence!

Why exactly this happens is up for debate. Science vs Spirituality… the oldest debate of our time. I personally like to blend them both, to get the best of both worlds. When I was a Holistic Health Coach specializing in thyroid and hormones, I learned in my studies that the full moon quite literally dehydrates us, and a dehydrated brain doesn't think straight.

Our bodies are made up of over 70% water. If the moon pulls the tides, especially when it's full, does that mean it pulls water from us? Science points to yes. When we are dehydrated, our body doesn't operate at full capacity, especially our brain. If we do not have clarity on our mental abilities to think, speak, or act, then throw in vices such as caffeine or alcohol to further dehydrate us… chaos ensues.

We have miscommunications. We crave sugar and salt to combat the hidden threat of dehydration and mood swings. It's a mess! So yes, what I'm saying is take extra caution in hydrating yourself during a full moon.

The spiritual side of this is a fun one. In my years of hosting Lightworkers Lounge and coaching hundreds of people, I have noticed that the full moon always does something to our subconscious. The next time the moon is full, ask someone in the morning what their dreams were like last night. You'll more than likely get a mouthful. Or, ask a friend who has been on their mind a lot lately. A lover from the past? A parent they recently lost?

The full moon acts as a flashlight shining into our subconscious, illuminating everything we weren't aware of. When we are in any other phase of the moon, we can ignore it. Sweep it under the rug, throw it in the closet and shut the door to, maybe, or maybe not, deal with it later. But on the days leading up to a full moon, miss Luna wakes up and chooses *truth*.

When the moon is full, pay close attention to the symbolism in your dreams. The people that haunt your thoughts. Perhaps random song lyrics get stuck in your head? What are they? Write them down. The veil between other dimensions and the one we currently occupy is thin during a full moon. During these times we have more access than usual to profound spiritual knowledge that can greatly make our journey here on planet earth a little less heavy. Normally the things that pop into our subconscious during this time are a whisper from the Universe of what, and who, we need to let go.

The Full Moon is a time to, once and for all, *release*.

Bonus: Fertility and The Moon

One of my favorite ways to use Astrology is to blend my past as a Health Coach with my present as an Astrologer to help clients with menstrual cycles and fertility. The Astro-Fertility information I've learned in just a few years has been astonishing. The blatant examples of how we are physically, emotionally and spiritually connected to the stars will never cease to amaze me. Although, as much as we know we are one with the Universe, why does it still sometimes surprise us when we are reminded of it through tangible examples like the miracle of conception? Everything is truly, written in the stars.

If you are a female with a menstrual cycle, as you navigate your way through the exercises in this journal, make a little note on the day you begin to bleed, as well as the day you ovulate. You'll be surprised by how much our body is telling us through syncing with the moon. I've noticed in my own menstrual cycle that I can be a day or two early or late depending on the moon. A lot of women report ovulating or bleeding on exactly a new or full moon.

There are two cycles that most women fall under: **A Red Cycle and a White Cycle.**

Red Cycle

This is when you ovulate with the new moon, and bleed with the full moon. This is a period of time where you are being called to heal your community. Emotionally heal yourself, so you can become the best partner, mother, member of society, that you can be. It is a time to transmute wounds into lessons. To work with the Universe on healing the collective. To turn pain into power. This is your time to focus all energy on creative pursuits and more masculine-type tasks, such as career!

White Cycle

This is exactly the opposite of a red cycle, and it's known to be the cycle of fertility. **It's when a woman ovulates with the full moon, and bleeds with the new moon.** This is the cycle that is most natural, and is a good sign that you are ready to enter the world of motherhood. You're fully in sync with nature! A lot of animals in the wild, or even humans who are able to live without the influence of any man-made commodities, typically fall under the white cycle. Straight from the farmers almanac, plants fare better under a full moon. They have more time to grow because they essentially receive more sunlight from that bright, glowing moon! What better time to release an egg and 'grow' a baby. Thus, what better time to shed the old uterus lining and begin a brand new one, than at the turn of a new moon.

*Ladies, please take note that fertility and conception is even more unique than a birth chart. This is by no means medical advice, and you should always bring serious medical inquiries to a trained professional. Also, many women have conceived while on a red cycle, it doesn't mean you

are infertile if you fall under this one. You can very well still get pregnant on a red cycle, so I would discourage using it was a form of birth control.

Now, take what resonates and leave what doesn't. I've seen many women achieve pregnancy under both cycles, and lately, I've been drawn to a completely different perspective on the Astrological art of fertility; the, 'Jonas Method'

Created by Czech fertility expert Dr. Eugen Jonas in the 1950's, he claims that women are most fertile when they happen to ovulate when the moon is in the same phase that it was when they were born.

There are many ways to find out what phase the moon was in when you were born with a simple google search. Simply put, if the moon was full when you were born, you should be most fertile when the moon is full every month. If you were born on a waxing crescent, you will be most fertile during the month when the moon is waxing crescent.

Interesting right? Be sure to add some notes about your cycle during your journaling!

Your Big Three

I've found it interesting at how fast our culture is shifting towards a keen interest in understanding ourselves through the stars. Perhaps we're all realizing the collective feeling we share of being fascinated by the moon? Or maybe it's just the age of Aquarius at work. Regardless, work up the bravery to ask a few strangers what their sun sign is; I can almost guarantee at least one of them will say "Virgo! and my moon is in Cancer and I'm a Gemini rising!"

To find your big three, you will need your exact birth time down to the minute. This is because the rising sign changes by the minute. However, a lot of times you can find your sun and moon sign without the time of birth, since the sun changes signs every day and the moon changes every 2-2.5 days.

Our birth chart is divided into 12 houses, or, pizza slices as my Taurus rising likes to call them. To say we are only our sun sign is like saying one piece of the pizza represents the whole; simply not true. Some slices have more toppings and resonate more with our taste buds. Others have too much sauce and don't sit well with our palate. Have you ever met someone who said something like, "I know I'm a Cancer, but I've always known I don't want children in this life." This person may have an Aries moon and Aries rising. Cancer, being the sign that rules mothering, nurturing, and family, may clash with the Aries energy of, "I want to do what I want, when I want without asking anyone for permission."

Perhaps a friend always sends you Astrology memes on Instagram and you think… ok, I know I'm a Libra but I don't flirt *that* much. *Yeah I may be a Capricorn, but I'm usually the life of the party!* The rest of their chart will hold the answer to this.

So, knowing your *Big Three* has become the new, knowing your sun sign. The next time you're creating a profile on a dating app, be sure to put your moon sign in your bio— Thank me later.

Remember discussing the three characters we play everyday? Life is like being on one continuous movie set, and we're the main character. We switch between three different costumes as we go on fulfilling our role; *our big three.* This is what they mean:

Sun sign: Our life force. Ego. When the sun transits a house, it brings attention to self, in that area of life. It's the foundation and core of our personality. The lens we express ourselves through. The sun represents the masculine energy in us, and it is the character we play when we're with our friends and family. People that know us, are used to us, who know our quirks. This is the YOU that you stand proud in, and show off to the world!

Moon sign: Our soul. The side of you that is reserved for someone you're really close with. Our moon sign comes out when we finally get the house to ourselves. It's our intuition and subconscious. What we need to feel safe. *The moon sign is the true test of romantic compatibility with someone!*

Rising sign: Also known as the Ascendent, this is our uniform. The first impression you give people. This is the character you play when you're meeting someone new. This is who you become when you're giving a presentation, an interview, getting on stage. This is also our highest self; the part of us that has an appetite for life lessons. The rising sign represents what we are rising towards in this life.

One of my favorite Astrology teachers described the big three beautifully:

> *"When I see you walking down the street, I see your Rising Sign. When you introduce yourself to me, I see your Sun Sign. When you invite me into your home, I see your Moon Sign."* — Malika Semper

Have you noticed that around the age of 30, you don't resonate with your sun sign as much as you did as a teenager or young adult? I find clients over the age of 30 start to really detach from their sun sign; all of the sudden the horoscope for their Pisces sun never resonates, but when they hop over to the horoscope for Taurus, their rising sign, it fits like a glove. This is because from birth until age 30, when we experience what is called a First Saturn Return, we are operating from our ego.

Our ego is our friend. Poor thing, it really gets a bad rep in today's new age spirituality. But our ego is actually in place to protect us. To help us develop a strong personality, with likes, dislikes, preferences, and distastes. It's the nucleus of our personality!

Once we hit our 30s, and experience whatever Miss Saturn had to throw our way to catapult us into *real* adulthood, we usually become a bit more anchored in who we are, and what our purpose is. We step into our higher selves, and bid farewell to operating from pure ego. This is essentially detaching from your sun sign and stepping into your rising sign.

Remember that there is an evolved and unevolved side to every placement. Since the sun sign operates mostly from ego, we typically tend to sway towards the unevolved side of this sign. For example, a Scorpio sun may be overly cautious and domineering towards their loved ones in pursuit of someone with pure intentions, unintention- ally causing serious emotional damage to both themselves and the person involved. A Taurus sun may be too stubborn and hesitant to embrace change, ending up frustrated at their lack of career and financial accomplishments.

The moon sign is pretty balanced, in that we can swing between embodying the evolved, and the unevolved traits of the sign our moon falls in. An Aries moon can have a short temper and stir up commotion everywhere they go. Or, they can be the greatest cheerleader for others and inspire everyone to get up and chase their dreams. A Cancer moon can struggle to be self-sufficient, and emotionally manipulate people to get their basic needs met, or, they can be one of the most nurturing people out there. The true, "mom friend."

It's all about how and where you direct your energetic currency; your emotions.

The rising sign is the one we luck out on. This is usually our 'higher' self, hence, the word rising. The majority of the time, we embody the higher qualities of our rising sign. A Taurus rising comes off as very trustworthy, gentle, grounded and compassionate. Much different than a Taurus sun, who can come off as narcissistic and closed minded. A Gemini rising embodies the art of 'connecting heaven to earth' with their gift of passionate communication, much different than a Gemini sun who may be too surface level to ever go deep or speak with authenticity.

Knowing your big three can really enhance the knowledge you get from moon journaling, so I would suggest before you fill the following pages, you get to know yours. This will reflect how each moon phase personally affects you, and show you what area of life is lit up with each movement through the signs. It really helps connect the dots! You can find your big three by having your birth date, time, and place on hand, and visiting **www.astro.com** .

Other apps I love for Astrology and Birth Charts are Time Passages and CoStar.

The Signs

L et's get down to business! The Zodiac Wheel. The 12 signs. *How* we express the energy. Let's break down what all those symbols and colors mean. I know, it can look a lot like a five year old's artwork when you first see your birth chart. I like to make it simple for even a five year old to understand, by breaking it down like this:

Planets = What

What energy are we talking about? If it's Pluto, where in your life are you going to experience the most transformation? If it's the Sun, what lens is your personality being filtered through? If it's Venus, how do you love, and how do you expect to be loved back?

Signs = How

How do you express that energy? The signs will point to how you express the energy of a planet. For example, if your Mercury is in Gemini, the way you think (Mercury) is very intellectual, curious, and fast (Gemini). If your Venus is in Scorpio, you may find yourself in love with (Venus) a partner who consistently shows devotion and that they can be trusted. (Scorpio)

Houses = Where

The 12 pie slices in a zodiac wheel are called houses, and each one of these represents a different area of life. The energy of a planet in a house is like a little arrow pointing to that area of life saying, focus on this! This area of life is important! If someone has a stellium in one house (three or more planets), it's a good indication that this area of life is their greatest source of growth, and with that, it's also meant to be their superpower. If the birth chart is a blue print given to us when we incarnate into this life, that area of life where the stellium lies is where they will be spending a lot of time mastering the subject. *If you put in the work, I often see people mastering the house with a stellium after their First Saturn Return.*

The signs are numbered 1-12. I like to explain it using the analogy of ages of children.

What is a one year old like? Brand new to the world. Everything is fascinating and magical.

What is a 12 year old like? Wiser. Coming into themselves and who they are. The big brother or sister, kind of getting tired of the family dynamic and craving socialization from another realm they have never ventured to (friends.) Also, starting to get sick of being treated like a baby.

Did you guess it?

1 = Aries
12 = Pisces

Knowing this, it's easy to equate Aries to having that thirst for knowledge. Everything is new! Fun! Exciting! Must try all the things! But also, steal my toy and I will throw a raging fit — red face, clinched fists and all.

Pisces, our number 12, is the oldest of the signs, and is frequently known as the old soul of the zodiac. A Pisces sun needs to be wary of falling too deep into pessimism. It's been said that Pisces people have lived previous lives as every other sign; they've been an Aquarius.

They've learned the Libra lessons. They've mastered Virgo. So in this lifetime, they are *so over it.* Can I move on to another Universe now? Said every Pisces.

Now that you have an idea of each number a sign represents, you can assign energy to each based off of the human age range. Thanks to mainstream media, and of course, our personal experience with each sign, people have equated some signs to being better or easier than others. But again, there is no such thing as a bad placement in Astrology. Pay close attention to this section, as having a general understanding of the pros and cons to each sign will give you a great insight into what each moon phase might bring up for you as you journal.

1. Aries

The young one. Wild. Bold. Here to run from person to person and wake them up! High level of optimism, because once one toy loses it's shine, we throw it aside and grab a new one. Once the ocean has lost its allure, we run to the mountains to climb. Follow the leader! Said Aries, as they wave a hand towards the rest of the signs.

2. Taurus

You know who was a Taurus? Buddha. And what does he teach us? The power of stillness. A Taurus soul is a sensitive one. All of their senses are so deeply heightened, they can easily get overwhelmed in our fast paced, over stimulating world. It's no wonder these sun signs are usually the one's who gravitate towards cannabis the most — indica strain, please! Taurus craves stability and routine. They will be the one to order the same latte with the same milk and 3 shots of espresso, every, single, day. Sensual, slow moving, and one of the most trustworthy signs, this is one of the happiest placements for the moon to be in. In the child analogy, a two year old will thrive when they have routine, their soft blanket, and the house is calm and cozy.

3. Gemini

The gift of gab! A child who turns three really starts to talk and think. Gemini's get a bad rep for being 'two faced' but this is simply because they are so curious about all the things, all the time. They want to eat at both places! They want to date both partners! Book a ticket to both places! They are here to learn and constantly be intellectually stimulated. They often suffer from knowing they are the smartest in the room, but unable to say it. The symbol of Gemini is one of the most powerful, as it's a bridge between Heaven and Earth. Gemini is here to teach us infinite wisdom, as long as they can harness their powerful mind for good.

4. Cancer

If Taurus has all of their senses activated, Cancer has all of their emotions activated — all of the time. Think of a child who turns four years old. They really start to understand and feel what happiness, pain, love, and anger are. They can begin to communicate how they feel. Cancerians are passionate people — sometimes to a fault— they can't help it! It's their gift in this lifetime. *To feel.* But sometimes the overwhelming feeling of…well… *feeling,* turns all that water in their sign into an ice cube. Yes, sometimes a Cancer Sun can be one of the least emotional people ever. Stone cold. Never cries. They just need someone or something to remind them of the warmth unconditional love can bring, especially the love for yourself. Cancer is a healer and nurturer for all of us. It's ruled by the moon, after all.

5. Leo

A natural born leader, and ruled by the Sun, Leo is a party favorite. Find someone with a Leo moon; they probably keep their front door revolving, so everyone knows they are welcome! Laughter. Drama. Fun. Board games. At five years old, a child really begins to step into imaginative play. Leo can really teach us how to step out in confidence, and just plain have fun. Just don't get caught in their jungle of drama. These people can attract more than their fair share of petty disputes and reality-TV worthy situations.

6. Virgo

Here the child is, at six years old, officially taking off for school. Learning what it means to make good grades. Virgo stands for 'virgin' for a reason; These people truly have pure intentions and just want the best for everyone they love. Perfectionists, Virgos can lead the way in showing others what tenacity and long term commitment creates. But, they can also show us what *thinking too much* can delay. These are the English teachers of the zodiac! Cross your t's and dot your i's. "I only want you to pronounce everything correctly so you don't look like a fool in public!" says the Virgo.

On their high road, Virgo is selflessly of service. They love a good fixer upper; yes, both in partners and work. On their low road, they suffer from anxiety and insomnia, and nit pick people in an effort to try and control every outcome, until they are depleted and alone.

7. Libra

I once read during my Astrology studies that Libra is the narcissist of the zodiac. They don't try to be! I can see Libra's raising their eyebrows just reading that. How dare anyone call them something other than lovely. Libra's came to this life to master the art of relationships. Marriage, Divorce, Friendships, Enemies, you name it. At seven years old, a child may begin to look at others with a different shade of interest they've never felt before. First love; so innocent, so sweet. Libra's came to earth to perfect the art of love. Libra's never intend to hurt anyone; they just don't understand the healing depths of what conflict can bring, so they lie to avoid it and end up doing more damage than the root of the conflict itself. They came here to learn independence while in partnership, and to master the art of *not* being codependent.

8. Scorpio

The sign we love to hate. I used to be in this club. Being a Sagittarius, I thought my neighbor Scorpio was too dark. Too intense. They had a stick up their butt and needed to lighten up. So you can imagine the shock and identity crisis I went through when I realized my chart was all Scorpio and 8th house. Now I love my Scorpio moon! Scorpio's aren't scary, they are just intense. Passionate. The only real thing in a fake world. They understand that while life has so much beauty to be enjoyed, there is a dark side to the yin-yang that shouldn't be optimistically ignored. When a child turns eight years old, they begin to realize that things in the world such as bullying, parents fighting, people lying to you... actually exists. Scorpio's typically go through traumatic events in their life, or some pretty serious things at the least, to embody their role as the alchemist. We need to learn to love Scorpios, and teach them they can trust us.

9. Sagittarius

If the Zodiac wheel was a classroom full of students, Sagittarius would be the class clown. The one always raising their hand, intentionally answering the question with a wildly incorrect answer just to get a laugh. Or, these people are sometimes the smartest in school, acing tests without even trying. By age nine, we're starting to develop what subject in school is our favorite. We're becoming a bit more brave, and taking risks. Our parents are starting to give us more freedom, and may even leave us at home by ourselves. Sagittarius loves the classroom; they are the lifelong student! But their true classroom is beyond the desks and chalkboard; it's the big, wide world where they never feel fenced in. Find a Sagittarius that doesn't love spontaneous trips, hasn't lived in more than three places, or doesn't have a stamp in their passport…you won't.

10. Capricorn

Uh-Oh — time to look at the report card. Here comes age 10, and with more freedom given to us at nine years old, comes more responsibility. This is the age children start to learn the importance of self-discipline, and making sure you do what the adults say. Enter: Capricorn. Next to Scorpio, Capricorn's have a rep for being just as cold and stern. If we use the classroom analogy, Capricorn is the principal of the entire school! The elder who thrives on both creating and maintaining structure. They love the classic American family. They love to build things. They need to love their work, and go home everyday feeling like they were productive. (And made a good pay-check, to support said American family!) A Capricorn's self discipline can't be touched; most professional athletes have heavy Capricorn in their chart because of their high tolerance for pain… both physical and emotional.

11. Aquarius

I almost put an exclamation point next to Aquarius because I'm always so excited to talk about them. It's true, I'm bias, they are my favorite sign of the zodiac! By age 11, children start to develop unique interests and find what talent or personality trait they have that sets them apart. As a result of this, they either feel part of a group of specialized friends (athletes, artists, etc), or isolated and alone; feeling like they don't fit in anywhere. Aquarius swings both ways — either surrounded by friends or completely alone. You will never meet an Aquarius that is judgmental, or uses the word 'weird' to describe someone. The most eccentric sign of the zodiac, they can feel like the black sheep of their family. We are in the Age of Aquarius right now, as you read this, so if you have Aquarius in your big three, or Saturn in Aquarius, pay close attention to Astrology and really hone in on your daily spiritual practice! You are bearing the torch on the front lines for collective change right now.

12. Pisces

We've reached the oldest age in the zodiac; 12. By now, kids are leaving elementary and heading off to middle school. Hormones are shifting. Puberty awaits. Some kids can start to feel real melancholy, at the inevitable loss of childhood. Not knowing what lies ahead in 'growing up' doesn't always feel good. Pisces feel a never ending thirst to go back to another dimension, to shift frequencies. Especially right now, as Earth is a tough place to be. They absorb collective energy like an emotional sponge. Pisces are deeply spiritual not because they want to be, but because they have no choice; their thoughts and energy naturally gravitate towards the things we can't comprehend. Pisces rules spirituality, mental health, any substance that 'shifts' your frequency (ie; mushrooms, ayuhausca) and hidden strengths. I know many Pisces who are downright incredible at art, but fail to see it in themselves. Pisces is the Yoga Teacher that heals us with their voice. The Reiki Master that makes us cry with swift movements of their hands. Beautiful, colorful souls. All of them.

The Houses

A 'House' in Astrology simply represents an area of life that the energy and sign of a planet shows up in. It's important to have a basic understanding of the houses, because when we're looking at what house the moon is transiting, we're forecasting what area of life is about to get a dose of moon energy. AKA, where the emotions are about to flow. What follows is a brief explanation of each house:

1ˢᵗ House

Ruled by Aries — **ME**

The house of me, myself and I. The first house is your identity. How you appear to the world, both in physical appearance as well as your aura. Does your energy light up the room? Or do you have resting bitch face? This is the house of us being selfish with our time and setting boundaries so we can nurture and care for *ourselves*. When the moon transits this house, we can expect to see energy towards our physical body, self-awareness, and personality. Who do we need to set a boundary with? Have you been putting on your oxygen mask first?

2ⁿᵈ House

Ruled by Taurus — **VALUE**

The house of money. What you value, what morals you believe to be true, and your attitude towards wealth lives here. The moon might light up this house and bring issues with finances, or a surprise windfall! It might also ask you to adjust your attitude towards money; do you speak kindly about wealthy people? Or are they "all the same." When the moon transits this house, we may discover hidden talents we never knew we had, or gain/lose a material possession.

3rd House

Ruled by Gemini — **COMMUNICATE**

The gift of gab lives here. The house of communication! It's all about the mind, both in what we preach and what we learn. Expressing ourselves through written ways. Teaching, speaking, listening, understanding. This house also rules short distance travel and our siblings. When the moon transits the 3rd house, expect to receive added energy in the areas of siblings, transportation, intellect and knowledge.

4th House

Ruled by Cancer — **HOME**

The House that turns into a Home; this area of life is ruled by your mother, or any female figure that raised you. It's the house of your ancestry, your lineage. This is the house ruled by the moon, so it represents what we need to feel emotionally secure and safe. When the moon is transiting this deeply sensitive house, expect to receive a burst of energy in areas of life such as, mother wounds, feminine energy, emotional security, home and family.

5th House — FUN

Ruled by Leo

The party house! This is the area of life that focuses on children, fun, creativity, and new love. It also rules the ego. It's your creative expression on the high side, and it's the house that can stir up ego-based drama on the low side. When the moon is transiting this fire house, expect to receive a boost of energy in areas of life such as children, fertility, creative hobbies, and romance.

6th House — HEALTH

Ruled by Virgo

The house we call, GSD; Get Shit Done. In life we must balance running errands, doing chores, showing up to appointments on time, all while taking good care of our physical/mental bodies and doing our best at work. Phew! That's a lot. These things call the 6th house home. When the moon transits this house, expect to receive a dose of motivation in areas of life such as diet and health, caretaking, volunteering, and relationships with coworkers.

7th House — LOVE

Ruled by Libra

Here comes the bride... The 7th house is all about love. Partnership. But partnerships of all types, especially one's with a contract involved; marriage, two people in business together, etc. It's the house of justice, fairness, equality for all. In my opinion, it's one of the most important houses, because who we decide to make our life partner will dictate how all of the other houses manifest in our life. When the moon passes through our 7th house, expect to have a spotlight on your romantic relationships, marriage, lawsuits, and contracts.

8th House — TRANSFORMATION

Ruled by Scorpio

The house of intensity. Look both ways before stepping into this one! This is the house of power, death and rebirth, and the alchemist. Once we master how to turn pain into appreciation, poison into medicine, only then have we mastered the 8th house lessons. It also rules transformation, inheritance of all kinds (talents, money, etc) and deep spiritual rituals. When the moon stops by this house, pay close attention to what's coming up in: joint resources, intimacy, sex, death and loss, and deep psychological healing.

9th House — EXPLORE

Ruled by Sagittarius

There's a difference between spirituality and religion, and that difference lives here. I like to refer to this house as the house of recess, because it's jolly energy feels like hearing the bell ring and going outside to play! This is the house of higher education, learning things through experience rather than lecture, long distance travel, and good luck. A cat has nine lives, and they all live in the 9th house. When the moon transits this area of life, expect to focus on international travel, higher education, freedom from restrictions, and searching for the meaning of life through religion or spirituality.

10th House — CAREER

Ruled by Capricorn

This is the house of Career. Masculine energy. Our public image. Our social status. It also rules our relationship to our father or any masculine figure that raised us. This house is about sticking to a commitment; starting a fire and tending to the flame for as long as it will stay lit. When the moon moves through here, expect to apply self-discipline in the areas of material success, career, relationship to father, reputation, and giving back to your community.

11th House — HOPES & DREAMS

Ruled by Aquarius

The house of dreams coming true! The house of the inventor, the person who looks 'crazy' at first but ends up being the smartest in the room. This is the house of the person who constantly raises brows, and forces us to see beyond what we were taught growing up. It's the house of the humanitarian; one who wants to leave the world better than they found it. When the moon is transiting this special house, expect to feel a lot of shifting around friendships, social media, reinventing your dreams, and tapping into the collective.

12th House — SPIRIT

Ruled by Pisces

The house of all things hidden. If we have planets in this house, whatever energy they represent is usually what we hide from the world, even ourselves. It's the house of spirituality too; our faith in a force unseen. God, the Universe, Angels, they all shack up here. Yoga, Meditation, 11:11, Crystals, Feathers, Animal Guides, Twin Flames, Synchronicities... they all call the 12th house home. When the moon is passing through this power house, expect to be fine tuned to your spiritual practice, processing sorrow and grief, craving 'frequency shifters' like alcohol, marijuana or psychedelics, and finding hidden strengths you never knew you had.

That's it — let's leave the classroom and begin!

After completing three consecutive moon cycles, you should start to have an idea of what each moon phase means for you. This way, you can eventually practice it by memory. I encourage journaling with the moon for at least 90 days straight, as that is when you can learn to alter your thoughts, *rewire your brain and energy,* to work in your favor during each sign the moon transits through.

How To Use

Before I wrote this book, I completed a full 30 days of moon journaling myself. Just to see if I could actually gain insight into the waves of my emotions and energy throughout the month. I figured if I could, I had a good shot at altering my thought patterns to work with the moon, and harness each sign to my benefit. Spoiler alert: after having the idea of this book in my mind for a while, I finally put fingers to keyboard after completing that cycle.

Since the moon rules our soul, our emotions, I thought… no better way to work towards a peaceful, balanced life in a never resting society, than by working in tune with the natural world; the stars.

Everyday I woke up and checked what sign the moon was in, then made little notes in my phone of how I was feeling and the energetic theme of the day as it progressed. Despite being an Astrologer and knowing how influential the moon and stars are on our psych, it was still so intriguing by the end to see the connection between the moon phases and my day-to-day life.

So, in order to drive home the point of this journal, on the following pages I'll share my personal experience with moon journaling. A look into my iPhone notepad. I hope it inspires you to make similar notes and connections, to ultimately make your phases less dramatic and use them to your benefit.

Steph's Moon Journal

November 7th: Moon in Sagittarius

Super happy today! Even despite PMS being in full swing. Jordan and I craved an adventure, to break up the monotonous routine we found ourselves in, so we booked an air bnb an hour down the road. Once we arrived, we played the radio, and went to an orchard to pick fresh tangerines. We wrapped up the day skinny dipping. He had never done that before! We laughed hysterically and took the most ridiculous pics. So fun.

November 8th: Moon in Capricorn

Spent all day on Zillow looking for houses or land. SO DETERMINED! Probably should have taken a break, got a headache from looking at a screen too long. Full day of work.

November 9th: Moon in Capricorn

Moody. Depressed. Feel like giving up. Nothing is working... nothing feels right. Need more self-discipline. More structure and routine. I really think my lack of these things is affecting my mental health.

November 10th: Moon in Aquarius

Felt a bit detached from my emotions. Which probably was a good thing, because we finally made a decision to move 6 hours north. I had to push my emotions aside to make the decision, because I know if I start to think about it too much, I'll turn around. Worked out beautifully. I believe this big move will help us towards our dream, even if we can't see it now.

November 11th: Moon in Aquarius

Happy 11/11! Woke up feeling optimistic, right before sunrise. Had a great nights rest. Instead of my guides saying run, they showed me jokes. Lighten up. Awesome, and monumental day — moving out of the motorhome for good. Big changes, to move us towards our dreams!

November 12th: Moon in Pisces

We both feel out of body today. Just weird. Sleepy. Tired. Out of it. Craving the Florida Keys (my dreamland) more than ever. Grass is always greener syndrome? Interesting dreams last night. Felt like playing dress up when putting clothes away during unpacking.

November 13th: Moon in Pisces

My partner and I aren't getting along well. He is making me feel guilty for something that never happened, but he is so sure of. Mental mind games. Buried insecurities scratching to get out. We both feel standoffish. Sometimes I wish I could close my eyes and transport somewhere else.

November 14th: Moon in Aries

Worst day ever. Ever! Blow ups. Both of us unable to control tempers. Saying things we don't mean. Ended the day saying fuck it, ordering pizza, (we never eat this) and having a good talk with apologies around the table. That blow up needed to happen to clear the air. Whew.

November 15th: Moon in Aries

Got shit done. Ran errands, took calls, paid bills. All with time to spare. Felt confident AF. Appreciate my partner for being real, honest, and vulnerable with me. We both fight hard for our love. Body feels great!

November 16th: Full moon in Taurus

Feel fired up to go after my dreams, and work hard to achieve them. Body feels in shape, comfortable, solid. Even though we don't own this house, we've really made it feel like home. We're good at that.

November 17th: Full moon in Taurus

Body feels full of emotions ready to burst. Sensory overload. But, recorded a great podcast and hammered through work while feeling the feels. Focused on loving my dog when I found out my friend lost theirs. Feel like I need to do a clean sweep of the people I have in my life. Their morals don't align with mine. They aren't at a place I'm trying to go. Under this full moon, I want to release my old values system, and learn to value myself first.

November 18th: Full moon eclipse in Taurus

Woke up nauseous. Couldn't sleep all night. Annoyed. Need alone time. Don't feel myself. What is wrong with me? Are people trying to help me? Or keep me chained to a life like there's. Feeling untrusting of many people I thought were close. Major epiphanies about myself. Saw dolphins jumping out of the water at sunset. New morning routine began today.

November 19th: Moon in Gemini

Awesome day. Nailed an interview. Gave one of the best birth chart readings ever! Really enjoyed the morning alone to be with my thoughts.

November 20th: Moon in Gemini

Great morning! Woke up with a fun song in my head. Felt easy today to decipher what is a productive convo and what is wasted gabbing. Nailed my composite readings today! Felt the need to plan a lot for the future. Bounced from app to app on my phone all day.

November 21st: Moon in Gemini

Great day! Slept in, went for a hike, went to a cool new spiritual cafe and networked a bit. Came home and laid in the sun. Studied composite. On the phone with friends a lot. Great epiphanies with getting off social media. Awesome sunset with music… I am meant to make music, I can just feel it.

November 22nd: Moon in Cancer

Felt so happy to have the boys over for Thanksgiving! We had a fun time at the beach all evening. So present with them, nothing else mattered. They are family.

November 23rd: Moon in Cancer

Coffee date with boys was so fun. They may not be biologically my children, but they sure feel like it. It makes me so excited to add more children to the family one day. I would love to adopt, even. So present today I didn't even think about work. Family time.

November 24th: Moon in Leo

Lots of fun! Walks on the trails, in the woods. Made gingerbread houses with the kids, painted dinosaurs, wrestled, laughed until our bellies hurt. Hudson and I had so much fun dancing. Fun day with family.

November 25th: Moon in Leo

Almost had some drama, but we knew how to diffuse it quick. Re-train our brain to think different thoughts. Turning ego down and heart up. Feeling good but starting to wear down. Danced in the kitchen all night while cleaning! Shake that shit out. Watched a movie for inspiration. Slept like a baby from releasing so much energy.

November 26ᵗʰ: Moon in Leo

Woke up feeling a bit melancholy. Mood swings. Weird dreams. So agitated! Need to just call it. Put my ego to sleep and zone out. Too much fire today.

November 27ᵗʰ: Moon in Virgo

Woke up and talked in bed with Jordan for a while. Feel much better from yesterday's flames. Read Astrology over breakfast then made incredible love. Went to a coffee shop after and talked for another 2 hours. Great synastry chart reading in PM.

November 28ᵗʰ: Moon in Virgo

Whoa, forgot to even write this one. So scatter brained. Spent the overcast day exploring a new neighborhood. Might've found home. Got awesome, organic food at the grocery. Laughed and wrestled after dinner… so much laughter! A Virgo's sense of humor is so underrated.

November 29ᵗʰ: Moon in Libra

Woke up feeling sick. Whole right side hurts. Hmm, masculine energy. Discovered and realized I need an evil eye ring. "Return to Sender" energy, since my social media presence may attract unknown enemies. Not on my watch! Feel so tired today, but learning to accept that It's OK to rest!

November 30ᵗʰ: Moon in Libra

Seems all of my friends were in relationship crisis today. We are dipping our toes in conflict over here, but ultimately steering the ship away. Consciously directing energy. Must stop bringing up past partners.

December 1st: Moon in Scorpio

My mom arrived! Just in time for my lunar return. Everything feels happy, calm, right at home. It's interesting to witness my mother through new, grown eyes... what a transformation in us both.

December 2nd: Moon in Scorpio

Beautiful day with mama. Enjoyed nature, went to a cafe, decided that leaving her to watch the dog for over a week to be alone with Jordan doesn't feel right; I want to spend time with her. As a family. Not leave. Intense emotions, trying to process them all at once.

December 3rd: Moon in Sagittarius

Well, we made it! A full round of moon journaling. Today I had a lot of energy. Optimism all around. Went on a fun date to an interactive science museum! Felt like kids again.

Signs that felt good:	**Signs that need attention:**
Sagittarius	Capricorn
Aquarius	Pisces
Cancer	Aries
Gemini	Taurus
Leo	Libra
Virgo	
Scorpio	

How interesting, right? While reading my notes, did you make all of the connections to what I was feeling on a particular day, versus what sign the moon was in? Writing down which phases felt good and which ones need attention at the very end is important, so that the next cycle you can add a note to remember to be very self-aware and in your body during the difficult phases. Study the high-side of the signs you're struggling with, and implant the idea in your mind to move towards that energy. Just because you feel you've mastered some of the signs, don't think you're out of the woods! Some months, due to the inevitable, you may embody the low side of those signs. It will take a few rounds to really understand what each sign's "forecast" comes with, so keep practicing through enjoyed repetition.

Ok, I think we're ready.

Let's begin!

1ˢᵗ Cycle

The moon is in Aries

Date: _____   **Woke up feeling:** _____

High Side of this transit: Energy, energy, energy! Great physical stamina. Seeing the world through new eyes. Motivation to help friends and family wake up to their own potential while thriving in yours. Get outside and move! Release negative energy at the gym. Help the underdog.

Low side of this transit: Watch out for brash arguments. Don't start something you know you won't finish. Watch your temper. Are you listening to listen, or listening to react? Be mindful of letting your ego get too competitive.

Day 1 of Aries Moon
Today I'm feeling:

_____
_____
_____

Day 2 of Aries Moon
Today I'm feeling:

_____
_____
_____

How can I harness the fiery, take-charge energy of the Aries moon next month?

_____

_____

How can I prevent something negative from happening under the Aries moon next month?

_____

_____

The moon is in Taurus

Date: _____   **Woke up feeling:** _____

High side of this transit: It's the happiest transit for the moon! The moon loves being here. Longer bubble baths. Softer clothes. Enjoying meals at home. Getting clear on what, and who, you value. Feeling secure in your relationships, and finances. Feeling very grounded. Have you been working hard? Now is the time to spoil yourself.

Low side of this transit: Stubborn. Very resistant to change. Over stimulation with everything from the smell of the neighbors laundry to the sound of your partner chewing. Could end up spending more than you make. May feel as though your current salary doesn't reflect how hard you work. Difficult to see someone else's point of view. Smoking too much weed.

Day 1 of Taurus moon:
Today I'm feeling…

_____
_____
_____

Day 2 of Taurus moon:
Today I'm feeling…

_____

_____

_____

How can I harness the relaxing, treat-yourself energy of the Taurus moon next month?

_____

_____

How can I prevent something negative from happening under the Taurus moon next month?

_____

_____

The moon is in Gemini

Date: _____   **Woke up feeling:** _____

High side of this transit: It's time to get social! Your mind will be sharp. Saying all the right things, at the right time. Your thirst for books, podcasts, any teachings, will be large. A fun time to write a letter, journal, and communicate. Teach! A good time to enjoy happy relations with siblings. Very open minded, you may find you accept sudden changes with optimistic adaptability.

Low side of this transit: Sibling rivalries on fire. Miscommunications all over the place. Anxiety, panic, nervous energy. Feeling indecisive. Knowing what you want to say but can't find the words. Spilling secrets and oversharing. Gossiping. Inconsistent and lacking follow through. Talking in circles, or unable to say anything at all.

Day 1 of Gemini moon:
Today I'm feeling…

_____

_____

_____

Day 2 of Gemini moon:
Today I'm feeling...

_____

_____

_____

How can I harness the witty, intellectual energy of the Gemini moon next month?

_____

_____

How can I prevent something negative from happening under the Gemini moon next month?

_____

_____

The moon is in Cancer

Date: _____   **Woke up feeling:** _____

High side of this transit: Beautiful connection with family, especially females. Feeling held, very nurtured by those you love. Healing conversations about the past. Take time to reflect on & revise generational patterns you may be repeating. Spend an hour cuddling a pet or someone you love — no distractions. Step into your natural healing abilities and nurture others.

Low side of this transit: Emotional intensity through the roof. Explosive fights with loved ones, especially family. Gaslighting and manipulation. Feeling misunderstood, unloved, like nobody cares for you. Clingy, and over-dependent on others. Mood swings. Unable to feel any emotions, because you've turned to ice. Victim mentality.

Day 1 of Cancer moon:
Today I'm feeling…

_____

_____

_____

Day 2 of Cancer moon:
Today I'm feeling...

_____
_____
_____

How can I harness the nurturing, healing energy of the Cancer moon next month?

_____
_____

How can I prevent something negative from happening under the Cancer moon next month?

_____
_____

The moon is in Leo

Date: _____   **Woke up feeling:** _____

High side of this transit: Ready to step out! Feeling bold, confident, and ready to speak your mind — no matter what anyone thinks. Creativity is heightened. Try a new hobby, you may find you're actually good at it! Talks of bringing children into the world, or simply enjoying the company of a child. Be the leader of your life. Take the stage, and know you belong there — just the way you are. Start that project!

Low side of this transit: Ego conflicts. Performing for attention, not for the love of it. Feeling insecure. Introverted. Just want to stay in when you know you should go out. Doubting yourself. Don't feel like you're good at anything. Petty drama. "What are we even fighting about?" Don't piss off the lion!

Day 1 of Leo moon:
Today I'm feeling…

_____

_____

_____

Day 2 of Leo moon:
Today I'm feeling…

_____

_____

_____

How can I harness the fun, confident energy of the Leo moon next month?

_____

_____

How can I prevent something negative from happening under the Leo moon next month?

_____

_____

The moon is in Virgo

Date: _____   **Woke up feeling:** _____

High side of this transit: GSD! "Get Shit Done" You may find your-self slaying the tedious tasks like scheduling a dentist appt, dropping off dry cleaning, organizing documents for taxes — like it's nothing. New year new me? That's the feeling we can harness with every moon in Virgo. She encourages us to hydrate and eat our veggies, while perfecting our daily routine to be the most beneficial to our overall health.

Low side of this transit: Disorganized. Worrying too much. Forgetting to show up at the appointment, because it slips your mind. Attention deficit. Nit picking our loved ones, subconsciously trying to control them because 'we know what's best.' Overworking ourselves. Nervous system dysfunction. Insomnia. Shy.

Day 1 of Virgo moon:
Today I'm feeling…

_____

_____

_____

Day 2 of Virgo moon:
Today I'm feeling…

_____

_____

_____

How can I harness the healthy, organized energy of the Virgo moon next month?

_____

_____

How can I prevent something negative from happening under the Virgo moon next month?

_____

_____

The moon is in Libra

Date: _____   **Woke up feeling:** _____

High side of this transit: Enjoying romantic love. Starting a new, healthy relationship. Making new friends. Having breakthrough, compassionate conversations with our partners that clear the air. Romantic dates. Getting engaged or married. Finding an awesome business partner with the same vision as you. Feeling inspired by other people's talents. Rearranging our home to fit our new aesthetic.

Low side of this transit: Infidelity. Lying, because you thought it would keep the peace. Annoyance with your partner. Relationship/ Friendship conflicts. Narcissistic tendencies. Realizing the pink bunny was the boogeyman in disguise. Adopting a fake persona for approval. Leading people on.

Day 1 of Libra moon:
Today I'm feeling...

_____
_____
_____

Day 2 of Libra moon:
Today I'm feeling…

_____

_____

_____

How can I harness the romantic, peace-loving energy of the Libra moon next month?

_____

_____

How can I prevent something negative from happening under the Libra moon next month?

_____

_____

The moon is in Scorpio

Date: _____   **Woke up feeling:** _____

High side of this transit: Being unafraid to face the dark side of your personality. Owning your shit. Turning around and looking in the eye of what caused you pain. Turning poison into medicine. Being the alchemist of your life. Receiving money just when you need it, from an unexpected source. Deep psychological studies. Friends telling you secrets. Tantric sex for a spiritual connection. Closing out karma.

Low side of this transit: Power struggles. Stalking your ex and their new partner on-line. Letting your shadow side eat you alive. Discovering secrets. Feeling overwhelmed by a controlling, manipulative person. Getting into debt. Starting a toxic karmic relationship. Obsessive thoughts. Guilt.

Day 1 of Scorpio moon:
Today I'm feeling…

_____

_____

_____

Day 2 of Scorpio moon:
Today I'm feeling…

_____

_____

_____

How can I harness the powerful, transformative energy of the Scorpio moon next month?

_____

_____

How can I prevent something negative from happening under the Scorpio moon next month?

_____

_____

The moon is in Sagittarius

Date: _____   **Woke up feeling:** _____

High side of this transit: Feeling like a kid again! Laughing until your stomach hurts. A stroke of good luck! Starting a new class for something you've been anxious to try. Traveling! Going on spontaneous trips that end up changing you forever. Immersing yourself in different cultures for fun. Good debates with others on the topics: philosophy, religion, and spirituality. Speaking your truth with unwavering pride! Enrolling in school. Publishing a book.

Low side of this transit: Being too blunt. Not thinking before you speak. Not taking things seriously. Taking a spontaneous trip when you don't have the time/money to do so. Can't get off your high horse. Eating/Drinking too much. Not committing to anyone, or anything. Ghosting people.

Day 1 of Sagittarius moon:
Today I'm feeling…

_____

_____

_____

Day 2 of Sagittarius moon:
Today I'm feeling…

_____

_____

_____

How can I harness the optimistic, spontaneous energy of the Sagittarius moon next month?

_____

_____

How can I prevent something negative from happening under the Sagittarius moon next month?

_____

_____

The moon is in Capricorn

Date: _____   **Woke up feeling:** _____

High side of this transit: Self-Discipline. Endurance. Feeling ready to make big moves in your career. Great relations with any masculine figure. Creating structure in your life. Having a solid routine. Asking for a raise, and getting it. Starting something that will not produce immediate results, but will prove extremely fruitful in time. Getting a second job. Enjoying a great reputation and sincere loyalty from others.

Low side of this transit: Bossy. Controlling. Working too much without proper breaks. Being too serious. Inflexible. Closed minded. Unable to budge on anything that might knock down your current life structure. Badass temper that stems from frustration. Feeling burnt out with career. Unhealthy relations with masculine energy. Public image being torn. Lying to push your narrative.

Day 1 of Capricorn moon:
Today I'm feeling…

_____

_____

_____

Day 2 of Capricorn moon:
Today I'm feeling…

_____

_____

_____

How can I harness the entrepreneurial, structured energy of the Capricorn moon next month?

_____

_____

How can I prevent something negative from happening under the Capricorn moon next month?

_____

_____

The moon is in Aquarius

Date: _____   **Woke up feeling:** _____

High side of this transit: Epiphanies you never saw coming! Feeling inventive; ready to step outside the box and try new things. Using foresight to help humanity. Feeling unafraid to question what most people deem normal. Coming up with new solutions to old problems. Showing people that strange can be normal. Meeting your new best friend, or seeing a dream finally come true.

Low side of this transit: Feeling alienated from society, as though no one understands you. Anxiety, from having so many thoughts you keep to yourself. Feeling as though the world is screwed and there's nothing we can do about it. Paranoia. Losing friends. Giving up on dreams. Diving too deep into conspiracies.

Day 1 of Aquarius moon:
Today I'm feeling…

_____

_____

_____

Day 2 of Aquarius moon:
Today I'm feeling…

_____
_____
_____

How can I harness the inventive, humanitarian energy of the Aquarius moon next month?

_____
_____

How can I prevent something negative from happening under the Aquarius moon next month?

_____
_____

The moon is in Pisces

Date: _____   **Woke up feeling:** _____

High side of this transit: A beautiful connection to Spirit. Undertaking new Spiritual practices. Enjoying cannabis, alcohol, psychedelics, in moderation and respectfully. Seeking help for mental health disorders, and uprooting the source. Yoga, meditation, crystals, all find their way to you. Enjoying the bliss that comes with alone time. Protecting, cleansing your energy. Getting inspired by music, film and photography.

Low side of this transit: Over-doing it on the substances. Letting 'Grass is Always Greener' syndrome ruin a good thing. Feeling like you need to escape this reality, because it's too bleak. Feeling pessimistic. Allowing energy vampires to suck you dry, and mental health issues to consume you. Over romanticizing people, places, and situations that eventually allude you.

Day 1 of Pisces moon:
Today I'm feeling…

_____

_____

_____

Day 2 of Pisces moon:
Today I'm feeling…

_____

_____

_____

How can I harness the spiritual, artistic energy of the Pisces moon next month?

_____

_____

How can I prevent something negative from happening under the Pisces moon next month?

_____

_____

You made it! Good job on completing your first cycle, journaling with the moon.

Cycle Recap

How did you feel overall?

_____

_____

_____

Signs that felt good:

Signs that need some work:

2nd Cycle

The moon is in Aries

Date: _____   **Woke up feeling:** _____

High Side of this transit: Energy, energy, energy! Great physical stamina. Seeing the world through new eyes. Motivation to help friends and family wake up to their own potential while thriving in yours. Get outside and move! Release negative energy at the gym. Help the underdog.

Low side of this transit: Watch out for brash arguments. Don't start something you know you won't finish. Watch your temper. Are you listening to listen, or listening to react? Be mindful of letting your ego get too competitive.

Day 1 of Aries Moon
Today I'm feeling:

_____

_____

_____

Day 2 of Aries Moon
Today I'm feeling:

_____

_____

_____

How can I harness the fiery, take-charge energy of the Aries moon next month?

_____

_____

How can I prevent something negative from happening under the Aries moon next month?

_____

_____

The moon is in Taurus

Date: _____   **Woke up feeling:** _____

High side of this transit: It's the happiest transit for the moon! The moon loves being here. Longer bubble baths. Softer clothes. Enjoying meals at home. Getting clear on what, and who, you value. Feeling secure in your relationships, and finances. Feeling very grounded. Have you been working hard? Now is the time to spoil yourself.

Low side of this transit: Stubborn. Very resistant to change. Over stimulation with everything from the smell of the neighbors laundry to the sound of your partner chewing. Could end up spending more than you make. May feel as though your current salary doesn't reflect how hard you work. Difficult to see someone else's point of view. Smoking too much weed.

Day 1 of Taurus moon:
Today I'm feeling…

_____

_____

_____

Day 2 of Taurus moon:
Today I'm feeling…

_____

_____

_____

How can I harness the relaxing, treat-yourself energy of the Taurus moon next month?

_____

_____

How can I prevent something negative from happening under the Taurus moon next month?

_____

_____

The moon is in Gemini

Date: _____   **Woke up feeling:** _____

High side of this transit: It's time to get social! Your mind will be sharp. Saying all the right things, at the right time. Your thirst for books, podcasts, any teachings, will be large. A fun time to write a letter, journal, and communicate. Teach! A good time to enjoy happy relations with siblings. Very open minded, you may find you accept sudden changes with optimistic adaptability.

Low side of this transit: Sibling rivalries on fire. Miscommunications all over the place. Anxiety, panic, nervous energy. Feeling indecisive. Knowing what you want to say but can't find the words. Spilling secrets and oversharing. Gossiping. Inconsistent and lacking follow through. Talking in circles, or unable to say anything at all.

Day 1 of Gemini moon:
Today I'm feeling…

_____

_____

_____

Day 2 of Gemini moon:
Today I'm feeling…

_____

_____

_____

How can I harness the witty, intellectual energy of the Gemini moon next month?

_____

_____

How can I prevent something negative from happening under the Gemini moon next month?

_____

_____

The moon is in Cancer

Date: _____   **Woke up feeling:** _____

High side of this transit: Beautiful connection with family, especially females. Feeling held, very nurtured by those you love. Healing conversations about the past. Take time to reflect on & revise generational patterns you may be repeating. Spend an hour cuddling a pet or someone you love — no distractions. Step into your natural healing abilities and nurture others.

Low side of this transit: Emotional intensity through the roof. Explosive fights with loved ones, especially family. Gaslighting and manipulation. Feeling misunderstood, unloved, like nobody cares for you. Clingy, and over-dependent on others. Mood swings. Unable to feel any emotions, because you've turned to ice. Victim mentality.

Day 1 of Cancer moon:
Today I'm feeling...

_____

_____

_____

Day 2 of Cancer moon:
Today I'm feeling...

_____
_____
_____

How can I harness the nurturing, healing energy of the Cancer moon next month?

_____
_____

How can I prevent something negative from happening under the Cancer moon next month?

_____
_____

The moon is in Leo

Date: _____   **Woke up feeling:** _____

High side of this transit: Ready to step out! Feeling bold, confident, and ready to speak your mind — no matter what anyone thinks. Creativity is heightened. Try a new hobby, you may find you're actually good at it! Talks of bringing children into the world, or simply enjoying the company of a child. Be the leader of your life. Take the stage, and know you belong there — just the way you are. Start that project!

Low side of this transit: Ego conflicts. Performing for attention, not for the love of it. Feeling insecure. Introverted. Just want to stay in when you know you should go out. Doubting yourself. Don't feel like you're good at anything. Petty drama. "What are we even fighting about?" Don't piss off the lion!

Day 1 of Leo moon:
Today I'm feeling...

_____

_____

_____

Day 2 of Leo moon:

Today I'm feeling…

_____

_____

_____

How can I harness the fun, confident energy of the Leo moon next month?

_____

_____

How can I prevent something negative from happening under the Leo moon next month?

_____

_____

The moon is in Virgo

Date: _____   **Woke up feeling:** _____

High side of this transit: GSD! "Get Shit Done" You may find yourself slaying the tedious tasks like scheduling a dentist appt, dropping off dry cleaning, organizing documents for taxes — like it's nothing. New year new me? That's the feeling we can harness with every moon in Virgo. She encourages us to hydrate and eat our veggies, while perfecting our daily routine to be the most beneficial to our overall health.

Low side of this transit: Disorganized. Worrying too much. Forgetting to show up at the appointment, because it slips your mind. Attention deficit. Nit picking our loved ones, subconsciously trying to control them because 'we know what's best.' Overworking ourselves. Nervous system dysfunction. Insomnia. Shy.

Day 1 of Virgo moon:
Today I'm feeling...

_____

_____

_____

Day 2 of Virgo moon:
Today I'm feeling…

_____

_____

_____

How can I harness the healthy, organized energy of the Virgo moon next month?

_____

_____

How can I prevent something negative from happening under the Virgo moon next month?

_____

_____

The moon is in Libra

Date: _____   **Woke up feeling:** _____

High side of this transit: Enjoying romantic love. Starting a new, healthy relationship. Making new friends. Having breakthrough, compassionate conversations with our partners that clear the air. Romantic dates. Getting engaged or married. Finding an awesome business partner with the same vision as you. Feeling inspired by other people's talents. Rearranging our home to fit our new aesthetic.

Low side of this transit: Infidelity. Lying, because you thought it would keep the peace. Annoyance with your partner. Relationship/ Friendship conflicts. Narcissistic tendencies. Realizing the pink bunny was the boogeyman in disguise. Adopting a fake persona for approval. Leading people on.

Day 1 of Libra moon:
Today I'm feeling...

_____

_____

_____

Day 2 of Libra moon:
Today I'm feeling…

_____

_____

_____

How can I harness the romantic, peace-loving energy of the Libra moon next month?

_____

_____

How can I prevent something negative from happening under the Libra moon next month?

_____

_____

The moon is in Scorpio

Date: _____   **Woke up feeling:** _____

High side of this transit: Being unafraid to face the dark side of your personality. Owning your shit. Turning around and looking in the eye of what caused you pain. Turning poison into medicine. Being the alchemist of your life. Receiving money just when you need it, from an unexpected source. Deep psychological studies. Friends telling you secrets. Tantric sex for a spiritual connection. Closing out karma.

Low side of this transit: Power struggles. Stalking your ex and their new partner on-line. Letting your shadow side eat you alive. Discovering secrets. Feeling overwhelmed by a controlling, manipulative person. Getting into debt. Starting a toxic karmic relationship. Obsessive thoughts. Guilt.

Day 1 of Scorpio moon:
Today I'm feeling...

_____

_____

_____

Day 2 of Scorpio moon:
Today I'm feeling…

_____

_____

_____

How can I harness the powerful, transformative energy of the Scorpio moon next month?

_____

_____

How can I prevent something negative from happening under the Scorpio moon next month?

_____

_____

The moon is in Sagittarius

Date: _____   **Woke up feeling:** _____

High side of this transit: Feeling like a kid again! Laughing until your stomach hurts. A stroke of good luck! Starting a new class for something you've been anxious to try. Traveling! Going on spontaneous trips that end up changing you forever. Immersing yourself in different cultures for fun. Good debates with others on the topics: philosophy, religion, and spirituality. Speaking your truth with unwavering pride! Enrolling in school. Publishing a book.

Low side of this transit: Being too blunt. Not thinking before you speak. Not taking things seriously. Taking a spontaneous trip when you don't have the time/money to do so. Can't get off your high horse. Eating/Drinking too much. Not committing to anyone, or anything. Ghosting people.

Day 1 of Sagittarius moon:
Today I'm feeling…

_____

_____

_____

Day 2 of Sagittarius moon:

Today I'm feeling…

_____

_____

_____

How can I harness the optimistic, spontaneous energy of the Sagittarius moon next month?

_____

_____

How can I prevent something negative from happening under the Sagittarius moon next month?

_____

_____

The moon is in Capricorn

Date: _____   **Woke up feeling:** _____

High side of this transit: Self-Discipline. Endurance. Feeling ready to make big moves in your career. Great relations with any masculine figure. Creating structure in your life. Having a solid routine. Asking for a raise, and getting it. Starting something that will not produce immediate results, but will prove extremely fruitful in time. Getting a second job. Enjoying a great reputation and sincere loyalty from others.

Low side of this transit: Bossy. Controlling. Working too much without proper breaks. Being too serious. Inflexible. Closed minded. Unable to budge on anything that might knock down your current life structure. Badass temper that stems from frustration. Feeling burnt out with career. Unhealthy relations with masculine energy. Public image being torn. Lying to push your narrative.

Day 1 of Capricorn moon:
Today I'm feeling…

_____

_____

_____

Day 2 of Capricorn moon:
Today I'm feeling…

_____

_____

_____

How can I harness the entrepreneurial, structured energy of the Capricorn moon next month?

_____

_____

How can I prevent something negative from happening under the Capricorn moon next month?

_____

_____

The moon is in Aquarius

Date: _____   **Woke up feeling:** _____

High side of this transit: Epiphanies you never saw coming! Feeling inventive; ready to step outside the box and try new things. Using foresight to help humanity. Feeling unafraid to question what most people deem normal. Coming up with new solutions to old problems. Showing people that strange can be normal. Meeting your new best friend, or seeing a dream finally come true.

Low side of this transit: Feeling alienated from society, as though no one understands you. Anxiety, from having so many thoughts you keep to yourself. Feeling as though the world is screwed and there's nothing we can do about it. Paranoia. Losing friends. Giving up on dreams. Diving too deep into conspiracies.

Day 1 of Aquarius moon:
Today I'm feeling…

_____

_____

_____

Day 2 of Aquarius moon:
Today I'm feeling…

_____

_____

_____

How can I harness the inventive, humanitarian energy of the Aquarius moon next month?

_____

_____

How can I prevent something negative from happening under the Aquarius moon next month?

_____

_____

The moon is in Pisces

Date: _____   **Woke up feeling:** _____

High side of this transit: A beautiful connection to Spirit. Undertaking new Spiritual practices. Enjoying cannabis, alcohol, psychedelics, in moderation and respectfully. Seeking help for mental health disorders, and uprooting the source. Yoga, meditation, crystals, all find their way to you. Enjoying the bliss that comes with alone time. Protecting, cleansing your energy. Getting inspired by music, film and photography.

Low side of this transit: Over-doing it on the substances. Letting 'Grass is Always Greener' syndrome ruin a good thing. Feeling like you need to escape this reality, because it's too bleak. Feeling pessimistic. Allowing energy vampires to suck you dry, and mental health issues to consume you. Over romanticizing people, places, and situations that eventually allude you.

Day 1 of Pisces moon:
Today I'm feeling…

_____

_____

_____

Day 2 of Pisces moon:
Today I'm feeling…

_____

_____

_____

How can I harness the spiritual, artistic energy of the Pisces moon next month?

_____

_____

How can I prevent something negative from happening under the Pisces moon next month?

_____

_____

Look at you go, completing your second moon cycle like a boss. Good job! Are you starting to notice how intimately connected to the moon you are? Wild right.

Cycle Recap

How did you feel overall?

_____

_____

_____

Signs that felt good:

Signs that need some work:

3rd Cycle

The moon is in Aries

Date: _____   **Woke up feeling:** _____

High Side of this transit: Energy, energy, energy! Great physical stamina. Seeing the world through new eyes. Motivation to help friends and family wake up to their own potential while thriving in yours. Get outside and move! Release negative energy at the gym. Help the underdog.

Low side of this transit: Watch out for brash arguments. Don't start something you know you won't finish. Watch your temper. Are you listening to listen, or listening to react? Be mindful of letting your ego get too competitive.

Day 1 of Aries Moon
Today I'm feeling:

_____

_____

_____

Day 2 of Aries Moon
Today I'm feeling:

_____

_____

_____

How can I harness the fiery, take-charge energy of the Aries moon next month?

_____

_____

How can I prevent something negative from happening under the Aries moon next month?

_____

_____

The moon is in Taurus

Date: _____   **Woke up feeling:** _____

High side of this transit: It's the happiest transit for the moon! The moon loves being here. Longer bubble baths. Softer clothes. Enjoying meals at home. Getting clear on what, and who, you value. Feeling secure in your relationships, and finances. Feeling very grounded. Have you been working hard? Now is the time to spoil yourself.

Low side of this transit: Stubborn. Very resistant to change. Over stimulation with everything from the smell of the neighbors laundry to the sound of your partner chewing. Could end up spending more than you make. May feel as though your current salary doesn't reflect how hard you work. Difficult to see someone else's point of view. Smoking too much weed.

Day 1 of Taurus moon:
Today I'm feeling…

_____

_____

_____

Day 2 of Taurus moon:
Today I'm feeling…

_____

_____

_____

How can I harness the relaxing, treat-yourself energy of the Taurus moon next month?

_____

_____

How can I prevent something negative from happening under the Taurus moon next month?

_____

_____

The moon is in Gemini

Date: _____   **Woke up feeling:** _____

High side of this transit: It's time to get social! Your mind will be sharp. Saying all the right things, at the right time. Your thirst for books, podcasts, any teachings, will be large. A fun time to write a letter, journal, and communicate. Teach! A good time to enjoy happy relations with siblings. Very open minded, you may find you accept sudden changes with optimistic adaptability.

Low side of this transit: Sibling rivalries on fire. Miscommunications all over the place. Anxiety, panic, nervous energy. Feeling indecisive. Knowing what you want to say but can't find the words. Spilling secrets and oversharing. Gossiping. Inconsistent and lacking follow through. Talking in circles, or unable to say anything at all.

Day 1 of Gemini moon:
Today I'm feeling...

_____

_____

_____

Day 2 of Gemini moon:
Today I'm feeling…

_____
_____
_____

How can I harness the witty, intellectual energy of the Gemini moon next month?

_____
_____

How can I prevent something negative from happening under the Gemini moon next month?

_____
_____

The moon is in Cancer

Date: _____   **Woke up feeling:** _____

High side of this transit: Beautiful connection with family, especially females. Feeling held, very nurtured by those you love. Healing conversations about the past. Take time to reflect on & revise generational patterns you may be repeating. Spend an hour cuddling a pet or someone you love — no distractions. Step into your natural healing abilities and nurture others.

Low side of this transit: Emotional intensity through the roof. Explosive fights with loved ones, especially family. Gaslighting and manipulation. Feeling misunderstood, unloved, like nobody cares for you. Clingy, and over-dependent on others. Mood swings. Unable to feel any emotions, because you've turned to ice. Victim mentality.

Day 1 of Cancer moon:
Today I'm feeling…

_____

_____

_____

Day 2 of Cancer moon:
Today I'm feeling...

_____

_____

_____

How can I harness the nurturing, healing energy of the Cancer moon next month?

_____

_____

How can I prevent something negative from happening under the Cancer moon next month?

_____

_____

The moon is in Leo

Date: _____   **Woke up feeling:** _____

High side of this transit: Ready to step out! Feeling bold, confident, and ready to speak your mind — no matter what anyone thinks. Creativity is heightened. Try a new hobby, you may find you're actually good at it! Talks of bringing children into the world, or simply enjoying the company of a child. Be the leader of your life. Take the stage, and know you belong there — just the way you are. Start that project!

Low side of this transit: Ego conflicts. Performing for attention, not for the love of it. Feeling insecure. Introverted. Just want to stay in when you know you should go out. Doubting yourself. Don't feel like you're good at anything. Petty drama. "What are we even fighting about?" Don't piss off the lion!

Day 1 of Leo moon:
Today I'm feeling...

_____

_____

_____

Day 2 of Leo moon:
Today I'm feeling…

_____

_____

_____

How can I harness the fun, confident energy of the Leo moon next month?

_____

_____

How can I prevent something negative from happening under the Leo moon next month?

_____

_____

The moon is in Virgo

Date: _____   **Woke up feeling:** _____

High side of this transit: GSD! "Get Shit Done" You may find your-self slaying the tedious tasks like scheduling a dentist appt, dropping off dry cleaning, organizing documents for taxes — like it's nothing. New year new me? That's the feeling we can harness with every moon in Virgo. She encourages us to hydrate and eat our veggies, while perfecting our daily routine to be the most beneficial to our overall health.

Low side of this transit: Disorganized. Worrying too much. Forgetting to show up at the appointment, because it slips your mind. Attention deficit. Nit picking our loved ones, subconsciously trying to control them because 'we know what's best.' Overworking ourselves. Nervous system dysfunction. Insomnia. Shy.

Day 1 of Virgo moon:
Today I'm feeling…

_____

_____

_____

Day 2 of Virgo moon:
Today I'm feeling...

_____
_____
_____

How can I harness the healthy, organized energy of the Virgo moon next month?

_____
_____

How can I prevent something negative from happening under the Virgo moon next month?

_____
_____

The moon is in Libra

Date: _____ **Woke up feeling:** _____

High side of this transit: Enjoying romantic love. Starting a new, healthy relationship. Making new friends. Having breakthrough, compassionate conversations with our partners that clear the air. Romantic dates. Getting engaged or married. Finding an awesome business partner with the same vision as you. Feeling inspired by other people's talents. Rearranging our home to fit our new aesthetic.

Low side of this transit: Infidelity. Lying, because you thought it would keep the peace. Annoyance with your partner. Relationship/ Friendship conflicts. Narcissistic tendencies. Realizing the pink bunny was the boogeyman in disguise. Adopting a fake persona for approval. Leading people on.

Day 1 of Libra moon:
Today I'm feeling…

_____

_____

_____

Day 2 of Libra moon:
Today I'm feeling...

_____

_____

_____

How can I harness the romantic, peace-loving energy of the Libra moon next month?

_____

_____

How can I prevent something negative from happening under the Libra moon next month?

_____

_____

The moon is in Scorpio

Date: _____   **Woke up feeling:** _____

High side of this transit: Being unafraid to face the dark side of your personality. Owning your shit. Turning around and looking in the eye of what caused you pain. Turning poison into medicine. Being the alchemist of your life. Receiving money just when you need it, from an unexpected source. Deep psychological studies. Friends telling you secrets. Tantric sex for a spiritual connection. Closing out karma.

Low side of this transit: Power struggles. Stalking your ex and their new partner on-line. Letting your shadow side eat you alive. Discovering secrets. Feeling overwhelmed by a controlling, manipulative person. Getting into debt. Starting a toxic karmic relationship. Obsessive thoughts. Guilt.

Day 1 of Scorpio moon:
Today I'm feeling...

_____

_____

_____

Day 2 of Scorpio moon:
Today I'm feeling…

_____

_____

_____

How can I harness the powerful, transformative energy of the Scorpio moon next month?

_____

_____

How can I prevent something negative from happening under the Scorpio moon next month?

_____

_____

The moon is in Sagittarius

Date: _____   **Woke up feeling:** _____

High side of this transit: Feeling like a kid again! Laughing until your stomach hurts. A stroke of good luck! Starting a new class for something you've been anxious to try. Traveling! Going on spontaneous trips that end up changing you forever. Immersing yourself in different cultures for fun. Good debates with others on the topics: philosophy, religion, and spirituality. Speaking your truth with unwavering pride! Enrolling in school. Publishing a book.

Low side of this transit: Being too blunt. Not thinking before you speak. Not taking things seriously. Taking a spontaneous trip when you don't have the time/money to do so. Can't get off your high horse. Eating/Drinking too much. Not committing to anyone, or anything. Ghosting people.

Day 1 of Sagittarius moon:
Today I'm feeling…

_____

_____

_____

Day 2 of Sagittarius moon:
Today I'm feeling…

_____

_____

_____

How can I harness the optimistic, spontaneous energy of the Sagittarius moon next month?

_____

_____

How can I prevent something negative from happening under the Sagittarius moon next month?

_____

_____

The moon is in Capricorn

Date: _____   **Woke up feeling:** _____

High side of this transit: Self-Discipline. Endurance. Feeling ready to make big moves in your career. Great relations with any masculine figure. Creating structure in your life. Having a solid routine. Asking for a raise, and getting it. Starting something that will not produce immediate results, but will prove extremely fruitful in time. Getting a second job. Enjoying a great reputation and sincere loyalty from others.

Low side of this transit: Bossy. Controlling. Working too much without proper breaks. Being too serious. Inflexible. Closed minded. Unable to budge on anything that might knock down your current life structure. Badass temper that stems from frustration. Feeling burnt out with career. Unhealthy relations with masculine energy. Public image being torn. Lying to push your narrative.

Day 1 of Capricorn moon:
Today I'm feeling…

_____

_____

_____

Day 2 of Capricorn moon:
Today I'm feeling…

_____

_____

_____

How can I harness the entrepreneurial, structured energy of the Capricorn moon next month?

_____

_____

How can I prevent something negative from happening under the Capricorn moon next month?

_____

_____

The moon is in Aquarius

Date: _____   **Woke up feeling:** _____

High side of this transit: Epiphanies you never saw coming! Feeling inventive; ready to step outside the box and try new things. Using foresight to help humanity. Feeling unafraid to question what most people deem normal. Coming up with new solutions to old problems. Showing people that strange can be normal. Meeting your new best friend, or seeing a dream finally come true.

Low side of this transit: Feeling alienated from society, as though no one understands you. Anxiety, from having so many thoughts you keep to yourself. Feeling as though the world is screwed and there's nothing we can do about it. Paranoia. Losing friends. Giving up on dreams. Diving too deep into conspiracies.

Day 1 of Aquarius moon:
Today I'm feeling...

_____
_____
_____

Day 2 of Aquarius moon:
Today I'm feeling…

_____

_____

_____

How can I harness the inventive, humanitarian energy of the Aquarius moon next month?

_____

_____

How can I prevent something negative from happening under the Aquarius moon next month?

_____

_____

The moon is in Pisces

Date: _____   **Woke up feeling:** _____

High side of this transit: A beautiful connection to Spirit. Undertaking new Spiritual practices. Enjoying cannabis, alcohol, psychedelics, in moderation and respectfully. Seeking help for mental health disorders, and uprooting the source. Yoga, meditation, crystals, all find their way to you. Enjoying the bliss that comes with alone time. Protecting, cleansing your energy. Getting inspired by music, film and photography.

Low side of this transit: Over-doing it on the substances. Letting 'Grass is Always Greener' syndrome ruin a good thing. Feeling like you need to escape this reality, because it's too bleak. Feeling pessimistic. Allowing energy vampires to suck you dry, and mental health issues to consume you. Over romanticizing people, places, and situations that eventually allude you.

Day 1 of Pisces moon:
Today I'm feeling…

_____

_____

_____

Day 2 of Pisces moon:
Today I'm feeling…

_____

_____

_____

How can I harness the spiritual, artistic energy of the Pisces moon next month?

_____

_____

How can I prevent something negative from happening under the Pisces moon next month?

_____

_____

Tic-Tac-Toe, three in a row! I can't believe we just spent an entire season together.

Did we watch the leaves change in Fall, journaling how you felt each day to the smell of a campfire?

Did you journal with a thunderstorm in Summer, splashes of warm rain on the pages?

Did you cozy up with this book to pass time in Winter, dropping crumbs in the spine from some carb-laden goodie leftover from holidays?

Or did you bloom into an entire new person using this journal in Spring, the first warm breeze coming through the window as you turn a page.

Either way, I'm really proud of you for tapping into Earth energy and staying consistent with this.

Well, how do you feel? Which signs have you mastered?

_____

_____

_____

Signs that felt good:

Signs that still need some work:

Saying our Goodbyes

A lthough we may never meet in the 3D world, I want to thank you for devoting your hard earned money and precious time to **It's Just a Phase.** As I wrote this book, I imagined us sitting together at your kitchen table, or snuggled in soft blankets on your couch, sifting through this journal, having "*ah-ha!*" moments that lit our eyes with realizations. Like a child gleaming on Easter morning after finding the first egg, I imagined us finding the 'easter eggs' of our mind — mental connections to solve subconscious patterns that have been keeping us tied to old ways, too long. The ever-joyful realization that we just found the key to unlock us from our own, self imposed prison.

I wrote this book from an air bnb on a beach in Panama City, Florida, living a life of abundance that no one in my lineage has ever seen. From working a 9-5 in a cold, lifeless cubicle, to writing about the stars on a warm, white-sand beach; please let me be living proof that with a little self-discipline and mental rewiring, you can manifest anything your mind decides to.

I created my current reality by working with psychology, spirituality, and most importantly, the stars. Astrology: It is such a profound treasure that I wish everyone had an open mind to, because like a weather forecast, it can help us prepare and be centered through the eye of the inevitable storm.

This book was written with the intent to help everyone remain in their internal locus of control. Understanding that their external environment can not hold a candle to their inner source of peace. But hey, I know just as much as anyone, if not more, how difficult traversing this current world can be. Over stimulation at every turn, hurt children disguised as adults projecting their wounds onto you. This shit ain't easy, but it's also not going anywhere. The best we can do is learn to navigate through it; arm our ships with shields and supplies to not go under with the blow.

My wish is that you come back to this workbook whenever you get knocked off your center. Your roots to remain grounded are always accessible to you... it's just a matter of taking a deep breath, and reconnecting.

Sending love from Florida and beyond!

—Stephanie

Notes